when the critic sleeps

pear urushima

Copyright © 2024 Pear Urushima

ALL RIGHTS RESERVED

Permission in writing from the publisher is required if you wish to reproduce, translate, or distribute any part of the book's content. The use of brief quotations embodied in friendly-toned critical reviews is welcome, along with proper citations.

Slow Drum Press
hello@slowdrumpress.com

Book design by Nuno Moreira, NMDESIGN
Photographs by Pear Urushima

ISBN hardback: 979-8-9916050-0-7
ISBN paperback: 979-8-9916050-1-4
ISBN e-book: 979-8-9916050-2-1

when the critic sleeps

poems that escaped the censor

pear urushima

SLOW DRUM PRESS

The best defense
Against the inner critic
Is gratitude

UNFOLDINGS

In me, there is a sea	11
Poet's manifesto	15

UNHEARD OF
The me I never thought I'd be

A poem about starting to write poetry again	19
The listener	20
Today's advisory	22
If not now	24
When pretty died	26
Haiku	27
If only, my dear America	28
Change me	30

PROMPTED
It began with a writing prompt

I'm from	35
Prayer in my top drawer	37
Ways to be alone	39
Today's lesson is	42
A practice in diction	44
Wabi-sabi	46
When you write enough obituaries	47

ENTRAPMENTS

Untangling everyday cogitations

Burden or privilege	53
Maybe later	54
Words	55
Less than	56
Left out	58
Anxious	59
Dreadful	61
Monikers	62

OFF BEAT. OUT LOUD.

Poems by a shy person who drums

Artist hands	67
Unravelings	68
I am a taiko artist	70
Mother drum	73
Tsunami of light	74
Taking flight	77
Oneness	80
Born this way	83

EDGES

Traversing the edges… some deep, some scary, some peculiar

Is this me	89
What if	92
Curtains	95
Rugs and shame	97
Paranoia	99
Fleshless	101
Saboteur's lament	103
The gathering	104
The path of gratitude	106
WITH GRATEFUL THANKS	109

IN ME, THERE IS A SEA

What you're holding in your hands is nothing short of a miracle. I like to write poetry because I've always enjoyed playing with words, but I don't like sharing personal things about me. The thought of risking exposure to potential criticism—both my own and that of the outside world—felt like too great a hurdle. By being a loyal warden of my poems, I believed I was safeguarding my self-esteem.

To compound my vulnerability, I come from a quiet and passive culture to which I am very loyal. I wasn't aware of any American-born Japanese women writers and poets like me who had made names for themselves. This absence of role models only deepened my desire to keep my writing hidden.

By all accounts, this poetry collection was never intended to see the light of day. I was determined to keep my writing safe within mounds of notebooks, journals, and the depths of my computer. Decades later, I yielded to the voice within me that yearned to be heard. It was time to be seen and take a chance. The part of me that wanted to take credit for being a writer and a poet finally received a long-awaited permission slip.

This publishing project started with a sense of deep gratitude towards my inner critic, my perfectionist, and my saboteur for their relentless efforts. After silently thanking them, I muted their voices until the manuscript gained momentum. The offerings you're about to encounter emerged timidly, yet with conviction, from the sea in my soul onto the pages of this book. I invite you to feel the ebb and flow of my poetic wayfaring.

Pear U.

POET'S MANIFESTO

To articulate every word, phrase, and line with much care and attention to beauty.

To pay close attention to the dalliances, dreams, and desires of my soul because they are the source of my aliveness.

To be mindful only humans can write poetry and to not take it for granted.

To be serious about the craft and not so serious about perfecting it.

To enjoy every turn of the line, the ending of one, and the beginning of the next and the next and the next…

UNHEARD OF

The me I never thought I'd be

A POEM ABOUT STARTING TO WRITE POETRY AGAIN

There was a loveliness to this moment
A soft kiss of insight
Unexpected, gentle and kind, yet
Disruptive, even perhaps life changing

Should I give permission
To my dominant hand
Fingers that have written thousands
Of words except for the ones dying to be written
before I die.

In a subtle act of grace's intent
I reach for a pen
And begin to write a stream of words
On lily white pages
Open and expansive
Welcoming me, home.
A thought.

Broken promises
Rotted dreams left to lapse and corrode
Is this your best life?

PEAR URUSHIMA

THE LISTENER

It's the noblest of all jobs
Yet one of the hardest
Perhaps unheralded, unsung

That of being a true listener.

One who hears you without
Filters and judgement and false interpretations
Taking in your words, inflections, and exasperations
As you speak about your friends and foes
Those you trust and those who betrayed you
Life's ups and downs, both frivolous and fierce.

At the end of it all it could be hours
And yet the listener's only response is
How worthy, kind, generous, and brave you are
Which they express with all due sincerity

WHEN THE CRITIC SLEEPS

And you
With humbleness and grace
Recognize the rarity of this moment
And say the two most important words
The listener wants to hear

Thank you.

TODAY'S ADVISORY

Don't leave empty handed
Your last breath will decide
When you've had enough.

Till then
Take your curtain calls
Daily.

Garland your minutes
With meaningful bursts
Of joy and things to be
Grateful for.

Reward yourself with
The accolades of self-care like
An inside smile, an
Intentional dodging of useless criticism

Don't cut a deal
To shortchange the chance for joy and wonderment
Don't let your limitations be your guide
Or they will sink you like quicksand.

WHEN THE CRITIC SLEEPS

There are no real rivals in your life
Only you,
If you allow your inner critic to be your foe.

May your attempts be high and frequent
Even frivolous now and then
Let courage carry you on its reliable shoulders

Make friends with the unknown
Because uncertainty is the
Great giver of life-affirming experiences

Accumulate a wealth of efforts, first steps, trials and errors
Even small attempts are valiant
And newsworthy

Appreciate that this
Very moment is a gift
That only you can activate

Your rigor will be rewarded with
Graceful coins you can
Toss into a wishing pond and
Watch the ripples twinkle
Into the night.

PEAR URUSHIMA

IF NOT NOW

By way of acceptance
    and passivity
        I do declare

Myself a victim of
    my own tragedy
        that of unactivated will

Hence, the native, raw, pure, and untethered
    inclinations
        bore no chance to breathe

Let forgiveness be my
    breast of comfort, my
        trustworthy savior

Where I cower quietly
    under a lifetime
        of indecisiveness

PEAR URUSHIMA

WHEN PRETTY DIED

Hair falls
silently
in restful clumps
while
wrinkles
defy me…
for now.

Meanwhile,
prettiness
becomes
a distant
memory
lit dimly
by the
tiny flame
of inner
beauty.

HAIKU

Black lives matter, not
Discrimination fears, not
Justice for all, not.

Brown eyes drip black tears
Bullets kill, no guilt, no shame.
Why is this normal?

Asian hate, fists drawn
Gentle people, harsh landings
Dignity over blood.

IF ONLY, MY DEAR AMERICA

Change your first reaction, beloved and privileged citizen of the free world
into a mindful
pause.

Discern…
Discuss…
Discover…
Defer…

Repeat.

CHANGE ME

Change me into someone
    with a wild and reckless will

Someone who
    highlights books until they're unrecognizable
Someone who
    couldn't be bothered with
        glares and stares, should haves and could haves,
opinions and suspicions
Someone who
    lives by the mantra
        "what if failing doesn't matter"
Someone who
    puts fun before fear
        coloring before othering
            dancing before duty
                play before obligation

Change me please, into
    that someone.

PROMPTED

It began with a writing prompt

I'M FROM

I'm from
>immigrants who made landfall in Washington, were called "the enemy", and
>>never complained

I'm from
>canned spaghetti and meatballs, bologna and rice, mish-mash and mochi

I'm from
>prim and proper words, clean and uncontentious words, safe and subtle words

I'm from
>asphalt basketball courts and Watts Towers, sand and smog, Bears and Bruins

I'm from
>two small feet that never grew beyond size three and a half

I'm from
>violin lessons, sheet music, LP's, and a radio blasting Motown and Vin Scully

PEAR URUSHIMA

I'm from
>high expectations, straight A's, report cards,
>>and square dancing

WHEN THE CRITIC SLEEPS

PRAYER IN MY TOP DRAWER

For the masala chai that I
really didn't want, but bought it anyways
as a social crutch.

For the wrinkles in the bedspread
and the iron in the closet
still in the box with the price tag.

For the cheap hotel pens collected
on trips that continue to be
the most reliable for writing my grocery list.

For the piles of unfolded clothes,
unsorted and strewn happily
on the clean, swept floor.

For the second hands on clocks
especially the ones that don't
make a sound as they make their rounds.

For all the thank you notes I received
and all the thank yous I said silently
to the recipients I never knew.

PEAR URUSHIMA

For the people with loud voices and not
much to say and for the people with soft voices
with a lot to say.

WHEN THE CRITIC SLEEPS

WAYS TO BE ALONE

Silence is golden. Be quiet.

Sing out of tune and flub the lyrics with so much confidence.

Write a letter with a real pen on a real piece of paper or even on, pray tell, a greeting card.

Prepare for loss, make someone's day because it may be their last.

Dwell in disorganization, embrace it, love it.

Wear the ugliest, comfiest sweater you own.

Talk to yourself in a kind voice.

It's not cliché, dream, dream, dream.

Make a fist and unfold it for 10 minutes.

Eat a spoonful of jam and double dip.

Laugh out loud, very loud.

PEAR URUSHIMA

Listen to music for an hour and do nothing but enjoy.

Draw a self-portrait of yourself with your opposite hand.

Think about death a lot, it will make you live.

PEAR URUSHIMA

TODAY'S LESSON IS

A bird's chirping, a traffic helicopter flying low overhead, garbage cans clashing as the trash truck maneuvers to empty them, all in perfect harmony.

A ride in a yellow taxi to an uncertain destination with a view on top of the hill.

A vista as far as the eye can see dotted with church steeples and rooftops with dogs howling into the night.

Uneven cobblestone roads, street vendors selling Milagros, and an orange sky that reminded me of my living room couches.

Hot water in a glass cup with no tea bag, no caffeine, no sugar, only a squeeze of lemon.

Thinking about what I'll be surprised by today, maybe I'll meet an astronomer.

Trusting the lady at the lavandaria to wash my clothes in cold water so they won't shrink.

Noticing that I twiddle and twirl my thumbs clockwise just like my mom does.

A PRACTICE IN DICTION

Other words for unlived.
1. Unchallenged
2. Unfettered
3. Deposed
4. Relegated to nothing
5. Hollowed
6. Pointless
7. Emptied
8. Surrendered
9. Unfated
10. Unbeholden
11. Disintegrated
12. Melted
13. Undreamed
14. Wilted
15. Decayed
16. Uncreated
17. Unbuilt
18. Deadened
19. Castaway
20. Felled

WHEN THE CRITIC SLEEPS

Other words for unloved.

1. Avoided
2. Excluded
3. Uninvited
4. Unworthy
5. Unnoticed
6. Invisible
7. Hidden
8. Underneath
9. Copacetic
10. Unreceptive
11. Detached
12. Single
13. Solo
14. Hostage
15. Waiting
16. Lifeless
17. Outlier
18. Peculiar
19. Missed
20. Tattered

PEAR URUSHIMA

WABI-SABI

How does one live with imperfection in a
    culture fixated on perfection and getting things just right?

How to be an achiever, yet make mistakes
How to be beautiful, yet natural, organic, free
How to be obedient, yet take chances

This is where culture meets tragedy
    the disappointment of not meeting expectation, of losing face
        for not even doing wabi-sabi correctly

Or maybe we just got it wrong
    and neglected to see
        the beauty of imperfectness,

That welcoming the blemishes that make us who we are
    and inviting the broken pieces of our lives
        to be re-arranged will only make us whole.

WHEN YOU WRITE ENOUGH OBITUARIES

When you write enough obituaries,

you finally begin to grasp death, the poignancy of life, the ticking clock, the countdown - even though you don't know when the final bell will ring, when the pearly gates open, no need to RSVP.

When you write enough obituaries,

The highlights of people's lives start to pile up and test one's self-worth - all the degrees, the endless parade of awards and accolades, all the great achievements, places travelled near and far, the list of grandchildren, in-laws with particular mention of their highfalutin careers - Dr. This, so and so Ph.D., a gushing of accomplishments is enough to kick anyone in the pants to get their life on.

When you write enough obituaries,

About people who've endured unimaginable pain and suffering for days, weeks, months, years on end, it's a wake-up call to stop waiting and living small, to make bold strokes, not timid ones, to take that chance because in the end, is there really anything to lose?

ENTRAPMENTS

Untangling everyday cogitations

BURDEN OR PRIVILEGE

To carry
    the dreams, desires, darings,
        dances, and delights
For the ones trapped beneath their heavy shields of
    coiffed hair, manicured nails, and shiny cars
        who call that a life
On bare, merciful shoulders, knees buckling like
    tired soldiers defending miles of unexplored frontiers
        mistakenly thinking,
"This is my duty"
    to be smaller than one's boundless ambitions, sacrificing
        meaningful contributions for a false sense of care.
If only to be aware
    of this human flaw
        disguised as love.

MAYBE LATER

Have I become a docent of procrastination?
Certainly, I'm over qualified, but
I'd be hospitable and welcoming, indeed,
Taking visitors through endless galleries of excuses
And mazes of soft seating allowing
For the most comfortable way stations
To sit and stare indefinitely at wall clocks
Ticking away the seconds, minutes, hours
Of wasted time as you occupy yourself silly
Mesmerized by screen after screen after screen
Of people, places, and things that have no meaning
To you other than stealing away the precious moments
Of a life gifted to you with no instructions only a
Promise of uncertainty and magic.

WORDS

There are words I don't believe
    I've ever used to describe my day
        At least not that I can bear to think of.

Words like sublime, splendid,
    unimaginably magical, wonderfully indulgent,
        heavenly beyond words, like a fairy tale,
            over the top, or "the best day of my life"…

Is it that
    I forgot that simple things can be deliciously rich
        and satisfying?
Could it be a fear
    of joy or perhaps thinking I'm not good enough
        for these moments?
Was spontaneity
    too big of a leap?
Did my tolerance for
    risk get the best of me
        when my inclinations knew better?
Or have I not
    stopped to reflect on how generously available
        a good life is.

LESS THAN

The worse
thing
about
underestimating
yourself is
acting as if
you
are
underestimated
which
could only
result
in
validating
your
undervalued
self.

LEFT OUT

Feeling
excluded
is an
unforgettable
experience.

ANXIOUS

Oh, how to extinguish the lingering smolders of anxiety
That bear witness to a nagging yearning for that
one moment when hardship changes your life

That life-changing notification about
a perilous diagnosis, a terrible accident, or an adventure
gone catastrophic

Which brings you to that moment of naked truth to
finally live the purpose you knew all along.

Funny how we create our own entrapments.

DREADFUL

My
biggest fear
is
his taste
in
furniture
will
be
absolutely
dire.

MONIKERS

Musical or musician?
Artistic or artist?
Athletic or athlete?
Teachable or teacher?
Creative or creator?
Starter or finisher?
Coward or courageous?
Half in or half out?
Accomplice or accomplished?
Follower or leader?

Please you or please me?

OFF BEAT.
OUT LOUD.

Poems by a shy person who drums

ARTIST HANDS

Artist hands,
> deep, parched crevices
>> intolerable wrinkles, stretched and quiet

knotty humps of joint, bone, ligament
> swollen rivers of purple veins

where a handsome story
> lies restless

waiting to be
> unfurled.

UNRAVELINGS

It began with a sound
swirling out of a bowl
singing crystals of light
to awaken their souls.

Curious and questioning
they wore coats of trust
vulnerable and willing
forge on, they must.

In unison they stepped
in diagonal stride,
not knowing their fate
would they collide?

As the cadence descended
bodies succumbed one by one
to the pleasure of patience
there was work to be done.

WHEN THE CRITIC SLEEPS

With hesitant smiles
giving way to the new
their bodies awakened
in movement, in truth.

Carefully they responded
forgetting their woes
what emerged out of doubt
was pure effortless flow.

I AM A TAIKO...

    A typical
    R eckless (I wish)
    T oo controlled
    I nhibited (at times)
    S pace painter
    T alented (arguable)

I am a taiko...
    A ging gracefully
    R uthless desire, yet
    T oo afraid to
    I nnovate and
    S tep
    T o my own beat

I am a taiko...
    A ware and asleep
    R adical and reticent
    T enacious and timid
    I nstigator and follower
    S teadfast and shy
    T erribly unsatisfied

WHEN THE CRITIC SLEEPS

I am a taiko…
- A lways
- R eady
- T o trace
- I maginary
- S pirals in
- T hin air

I am a taiko…
- A ppeciative
- R esilient
- T aciturn
- I mpeccably imperfect
- S elf-critical
- T hinker

I am a taiko…
- A m
- R idiculously
- T ired of being
- I nsecure
- S imply play
- T o inspire

"taiko" is the Japanese word for drum.

MOTHER DRUM

Fearless, humble drum

In your womb, my spirit wakes

Show me who I am

PEAR URUSHIMA

TSUNAMI OF LIGHT

I. How would you feel
    if your city no longer existed
    if the streets were gone
    if the buildings were gone
    if all the people were gone
    if all the noises were gone
    if the lights went out

How would you feel
    if your home was engulfed in a wave
    if all your possessions vanished into the sea
    if you had to stand in line for your next meal
    if nothing was left but memories

How would you feel
    if a wave washed your child away
    if your mother's arm slipped from your grip
    if your trembling hands let go of a friend
    if your husband or wife could not be found again
    if your pets and animals were taken by the sea

II. How would you feel
    if all you could HEAR was the black of silence
    if all you could SMELL was your home smoldering
    in the wind
    if all you could TASTE was the smokey air
    if all you could SEE was grief everywhere
    if all you could TOUCH was your own skin

III. How would you feel
    if you survived - alone, single, and homeless
    if you found the courage to lay the cornerstone
    of a new life
    if your imagination, curiosity, and will to live, came back

How would you feel
    if a tsunami became a bottomless ocean of compassion
    if gratitude had new meaning in your life
    if simple acts of kindness became the splendor of the day
    if you could appreciate a solitary grain of rice

How would you feel
    if you never lost hope
    and the light lifted you from the clenched fists of grief
    into the heights of peace
    forever

PEAR URUSHIMA

TSUNAMI OF LIGHT. This poem was written shortly following the massive 9.1 magnitude earthquake that shook the coast of Japan's Tohoku region on March 11, 2011, causing a tsunami of epic proportions, irreparable damage, and thousands killed and missing. Reflecting on the incomprehensible aftereffects of this natural disaster made writing this poem particularly challenging.

TAKING FLIGHT

You could hear the walls echo
a disquieting drone
soaked in indulgence
time left them alone.

Shapes painted by bachi
left not a trace,
but the beauty remaining
defied time and space.

Visions of pegasus
wings pulsing in air
unshackled their arms
with liberating flare.

Poetically they spoke
in 5-7-5
Haiku meets taiko
the words made me cry.

PEAR URUSHIMA

And then, little by little
the inklings appeared
quiet nudges of insights
Abhaya, no fear.

Whatever they ventured
good intentions were held
"cradled" in feet
where no one could tell.

By the end of this journey
they planted the seeds
transformation will come
with focus and simplicity.

In wonder, they departed
contemplating butoh,
where attention goes
all energy flows.

ONENESS

Fearlessly we surrendered
   in irresistible unity
      hearing the cry of the dance
         yielding with humble grace
            amidst tourniquets of canvas,
               indigo happi, and
                  sky blue netting.

And with eyes as wide as our ages
   we inhaled each other's trust
      and leaped...
         into a glistening pool of artists hands
            familiar, wrinkled, and soft
               splashing into billowy folds of kind flesh
                  buoyed by sweet meanderings of fue,
                     breathless beats of drum,
                        and the voice of an angel.

There we frolicked
   in ponderous cadence
      with winter faces and
         melting brown eyes,
            arms flailing in envious shapes

                legs trembling, weak and wondering.

Until the Light came
   and in one generous swoop
      lifted our weightless bodies
         beautifully distorted
            drenched in validation
               soaked with compassion
                  and dripping with gratitude.

Into the heights of peace,
   the power of presence, and
      the AWE-mazing feeling of
         Oneness.

ONENESS. After I saw a riveting butoh dance performance that depicted a family split and then reunited after the Japan tsunami, I was moved to write this poem.

"fue" - Japanese flute.

"happi" - loose jacket with boxy sleeves typically made of cotton and worn at Japanese festivals.

"butoh" - a form of Japanese dance, very very slow, avant-garde, imperfectly performed in the moment that developed in counterpoint to traditional Japanese beauty and symmetry.

BORN THIS WAY

i am
an
artist

irreverent
and insecure

radiant
and restrained

confident
and creative

spontaneous
and slow

aging
and afraid

inspired
and impeccably,

PEAR URUSHIMA

imperfect

i am
an
artist

EDGES

Traversing the edges… some deep, some scary, some peculiar

WHEN THE CRITIC SLEEPS

IS THIS ME?

The saboteur
who holds back in that
one split second,
on the cusp of giving life
to what terrifies me to the bone
harnesses my energy
strangles my being
that daunting thought of sharing
my opinion.

oh god.
the tension, the fear, the sweat
in that moment of decision
when the words form
and line up in a sentence
fenced in my mind's eye
where the guardian of shame
slams the door and says
not now.

PEAR URUSHIMA

In a crushing blow to spontaneity
how i mourned the chance
to reveal a part of me
dying to catch
the breath, the tone, the lyrics of my soul
and what could have been
a beautiful expression
instead
dissipates in silent
embarrassment.

Only to be saved
by the loyal understudies of truth
who thrive in playing the losing game
of pleasing
who so confidently take orders
from the people in the room
who've arrived with their own menus
who's agenda is
me first, not you.

Is this me
the impostor at the masquerade party
who looks like me from the outside
who impersonates me flawlessly
who pretends to be engaged and present in the moment
but who instead is wrestling behind wool curtains
stained in the regret and irony of knowing

WHEN THE CRITIC SLEEPS

there is a me inside
that is uncompromisingly
me

who desperately wants to smuggle in
any morsel of pureness
and stowaway to the cradle of
authenticity
where her fearless child can be rocked
ever so gently to sleep.

WHAT IF

In the pillows of my thoughts
I rest
Fearing nothing, but

Life itself.

I ignore the screaming whispers
shouting love messages
Inviting me to say

Yes.

The awkwardness of desire
wraps my body cold.
My swollen talents
bruise me from the relentless battle
of self doubt. Yearning for

Air.

WHEN THE CRITIC SLEEPS

I matter not to some,
but to the universe
who I attempt to fend off
with my impenetrable shield of

Shame.

In my next exquisite breath
rustling my blanket,
an indomitable force
cuts my throat with a sterile

Light.

And in discomforting surrender
I bleed a lifetime of
what if
I loved my

Self.

CURTAINS

At night's call,
the towering curtains of my essence
draw closed,
heavy and weighted
folds cinched by fear,
undulating fabric of furious
threads trapping love's yearnings
amidst monotonous patterns of doubt
sewn through the yardage of decades
where lost dreams wrestle with
maroon dye in futile, but noble acts
of compassion with nothing to
grip except for the hope of a
single stranded thread left to unravel
the desires of a pure heart.

The relief of the morning
accompanied by a family of leaves
tapping against the square window
of a slanted ceiling over the balcony
I look out to a feast of objects that have traveled
across the oceans and continents

PEAR URUSHIMA

Opening a door I embrace the simple pleasures
of a hot bath, then the embrace of a hammock
between two trees.

Until the day of reckoning
when God sent a
messenger to instigate
the unraveling of this fairy tale

Mystical, unexpected, perfect really.

The chivalrous man
with a kind smile
wondering, watching, waiting
for curiosity to edge out fear
just barely is all that was convincing.

Spawned by death,
crushed by a fall
into the moment
of destined connection
with the girl down the other hallway
who could strike a drum
but not say a word
who hid behind the
iron curtain
patiently waiting
for him.

RUGS AND SHAME

Oh here they come again
Bare, sweaty, soiled
Right, left, right, left
Stomp why don't ya
Easy on the heel toe
Have you heard of socks?
Crush my piles
See what I care
My tufts are getting old and grey
But I'm worn down
after listening to all the chatter
in this family den
the only thing I look forward to
is the vacuum, boy it feels good
to get all that grime off my chest
Oh it doesn't matter
I'll just get dirty again
With ground-in shame
The shame of being stepped on
Pounded under feet of
Careless people who just

PEAR URUSHIMA

Take me for granted
No wonder I feel
So ashamed.

PARANOIA

Our yellow throats, chapped, and choked
sat in the rear of class swallowing against backless seats
as the compressed spine of the nation
leaned forward and walked the plank of a seething
snow white tongue
hiding behind nicotine fences and posters inked with IOUs
walking the streets buckling beneath dumpsters of
birthday candles
pulled by war's leash with dog tags clanking
"we are not the enemy".

Barracks of pregnant fairy tales,
trapped inside endless miles of barbed wire
where a bully pulpit of doorless bathrooms
toilets swirling in tornadoes of spit and political grime
took center stage against a scrim of humble fog,
disarmingly quiet under the sky's black womb.

PEAR URUSHIMA

Then irony flapped its wings over the rising sun
and descended on a troop called
the 442nd Regimental Combat Team
who plowed valiantly head's down into a pool
of purple hearts
and swam amongst their brother's corpses, frayed and
naked to the paltry edge of hypocrisy.

FLESHLESS

May I name my child
May I mother my child
May I play with my child
May I see my child's smile
May I hear my child say "mommy"
May I hold my child's hand

Even if imaginary in flesh and form

WHEN THE CRITIC SLEEPS

SABOTEUR'S LAMENT

In praise of my saboteur
my ultimate destroyer
distractor of love
purveyor of broken promises
and the most
benevolent demon with
unwavering loyalty to
my soul's protection.

Let my endless gratitude seep through
your bloody pores
as I applaud not only your effectiveness,
but efficiency in convincing
me that I can't live without your
gatekeeping,
so dominant, so declarative
with my only regret being
how easy I made your life's work.

PEAR URUSHIMA

THE GATHERING

And there I was
seated cross-legged in the middle of my forehead
on the couch of my third eye
where wisdom lounges with feet up
keeping watch like a lighthouse.

I took a ride to my mid brain
Noting the ease with which
my long inhale carried me past
a blue highway of infinite knowledge and
vessels of deep red memories and longings.

In a brief moment I felt the bliss of being
and planted a crystal wish,
tiny, with ageless sparkle
in the rich soil of possibilities
a garden of soft, wealthy cortex
amongst roots of childhood dreams
to cogitate, coalesce, and create joyfully
into the night.

WHEN THE CRITIC SLEEPS

Then like the ocean's hands
reaching back to start another wave
I exhaled a beautiful breath and returned to my post
between my slumbering brown eyes
holding a symphony of cells, priceless and
translucent in my arms
with insights of a new day.

THE PATH OF GRATITUDE

On the path of gratitude
I walk
Every step
A blessing

On the path of gratitude
I stop
Every moment
A miracle

On the path of gratitude
I see
Every landscape
A painting

On the path of gratitude
I hear
Every sound
A symphony

WHEN THE CRITIC SLEEPS

On the path of gratitude
I touch
Every grain of sand
A wish

On the path of gratitude
I taste
Every drop of rain
Refreshing

On the path of gratitude
I love
Every person I meet
A friend

On the path of gratitude
I breathe
Every exhale
Freedom

WHEN THE CRITIC SLEEPS

WITH GRATEFUL THANKS

To all the poets and prose-makers, rhymers and rappers, lyricists and wordsmiths who inspire me every day by bravely sharing your work with the world.

To my trusty Mac, iPad, and iPhone—my essential technology that enables me to communicate, collaborate, and create at will. I never take you for granted.

To the wonderful team at The Tiny Book Course for providing the tools, guidance, and resources to publish this book with genuine kindness.

To Miranda J. Barrett, Hannah-Jasmine Brunskill, Stephen McDonnell, Gloria Mitchell, and Renée Schell, for reading the early drafts with great care, attention, and honest feedback.

To Anne Heffron, my writing coach, for your keen insights and steadfast encouragement.

To Dana Lutat, who introduced me to the joys of writing on Clairefontaine paper—the landing pad for many of these poems. Merci beaucoup, mon ami.

To PJ Hirabayashi, who taught me that "where intention goes, energy flows," a lesson I took to heart while writing this book.

To my mom, family, friends, and all who came before me.

PEAR URUSHIMA

is a writer, poet, drummer, filmmaker, storyteller, and producer. She's a Los Angeles native, living in northern California. *When The Critic Sleeps* is her first self-published book by Slow Drum Press.

Artwork by family and friends of Pear Urushima.

Ode to the poet

*To the one, both cowardly and confident, insecure
and indignant,
An architect of words built on a scaffold, often wobbly, forever trusted,
Tackling the most noble of tasks,
Care of the heart, purveyor of the soul, expression of Self.*

Ode to the poet

*To the one who dwells in the nonsensical, the whimsical, and the muck
of the unresolved
To the one who cries in and out of rhymes, broken lines, truths and lies
To the one who can't face another day without the promise
of wonderment and escape every poem holds.*

www.ingramcontent.com/pod-product-compliance
Lightning Source LLC
Chambersburg PA
CBHW030447100526
44580CB00002B/22